P9-CPZ-528

The Home Front Handbook

How to Support Missions Behind the Lines

by Woodrow Kroll

BACK TO THE BIBLE
LINCOLN, NE 68501

Copyright © 1994
by
The Good News Broadcasting Association, Inc.
All rights reserved.

20,000 printed to date—1996
(1160-208-5M-56)
ISBN 0-8474-0895-7

All Scripture quotations are from
The New King James Version.

Printed in the United States of America.

Contents

103921

Introduction

Is every Christian a missionary? Not in the truest sense of the word. Only those who are sent out are missionaries. Every Christian is a witness, but the word *missionary* means "sent one," and some of us are called to stay.

However, in this booklet I am using the word *missionary* in its broadest sense, even for those of us who are "sent" by God to minister at home. We have a calling that is just as strong as those who are called to go overseas, but unlike front-line missionaries, most behind-the-lines missionaries have failed to grasp the importance of their calling.

If your image of a missionary is someone who wears khaki shorts and a pith helmet, it's little wonder you may not see yourself as one sent by God.

Think of it this way. Some missionaries take the Good News of God's love around the world; others take that message around the block. While God calls some Christians to vocational ministry as front-line missionaries, He calls the rest of us to faithful ministry behind the lines.

It's for all of us who aren't vocational "sent ones" that this book is written. We may be behind-the-lines warriors, but we are warriors nonetheless. *The Home Front Handbook* focuses on ten unique and exciting opportunities to support missions behind the lines.

Somewhere in these ten opportunities you will find yourself— maybe in more than one. Discover your importance to God as a behind-the-lines missionary, and be faithful to Him in each avenue of missionary service that He opens to you.

Chapter 1

Be Active in Witnessing

Behind-the-lines missionaries see as their first duty to tell their world about Jesus Christ. That is witnessing. Your first opportunity as a behind-the-lines missionary is telling your family and friends what Jesus has done for you.

Why witness?

We all know we should witness, but do you know *why* we should witness for the Lord? Here's why.

1. Grateful people can't keep quiet

Do you remember when you trusted Jesus Christ as Savior? You could hardly contain your joy. That's what witnessing is—telling others of the joy that came into your life when you were saved.

Think of the story of the four hungry lepers who stumbled onto hoards of food in the Syrian camp. The Israelites were starving, and the lepers agreed it would not be right if they didn't tell someone about all that food (2 Kings 7). They were grateful to God, and grateful people can't keep quiet.

That's the way it should be with us. Evangelism is just one beggar telling another beggar where to find bread. If you have found the Bread of Life, gratitude makes telling others how to find Jesus a pleasure. After all, who wouldn't want to hear good news!

2. Jesus wants you to witness for Him

Jesus loved us and died for us at Calvary. Now He has work for us to do. He said to His disciples, "You shall be witnesses to Me in Jerusalem, and in all Judea and Samaria, and to the end of the earth" (Acts 1:8). Behind-the-lines missionaries are no less in the army of the Lord than front-line missionaries. Jesus made little distinction between the Twelve and all His other disciples.

In fact, not only does Jesus want us to tell our friends how He saved us, He places us in our neighborhoods and jobs for that specific reason. He said, "As the Father has sent Me, I also send you" (John 20:21).

Think about it. You have been sent by Jesus just as much as if you had packed your bags and moved to Africa. Right where you are, behind the lines, Jesus wants you to witness for Him. He wants you to tell your friends and neighbors what God has done for you and what He can do for them.

3. People need the Lord

The bottom line of witnessing is this: People need the Lord.

If your friends and family didn't have to worry about condemnation, Jesus wouldn't have sent you to tell them about salvation. But people need the Lord, and that includes people you know—people you vacation with, work with, go to class with, chat on the telephone with, etc.

The world may have many religions, but it still has only one Savior. Jesus Christ is that Savior and the only One who can fill the need in the lives of your friends and family.

So the next time you see their faces or hear their voices, don't forget—people need the Lord.

What's important in witnessing?

There are so many things to talk about when you witness to your friends. What's really important? If you want them to understand their need for salvation and God's abundant supply, here are the basics you should include in your conversation.

1. God's provision

I like to begin by telling friends and family how much God loves them. People need to hear that today. So many people think nobody loves them, but that's not true. God loved them so much He sent His Son to die for them.

God's love is everlasting (Jer. 31:3). He has always loved us, even though we sinned against Him. He didn't love us because we were loveable; He loved us because He is love (1 John 4:16). The greatest verse in the Bible speaks of God's love for us. John 3:16 says, "For God so loved the world that He gave His only begotten Son, that whoever believes in Him should not perish but have everlasting life."

2. Our need

We need God's love because we have sinned against Him. In fact, no one—not a single person alive today—is free from the stain of sin. The Bible says our need is universal. "For all have sinned and fall short of the glory of God" (Rom. 3:23). And our need is critical. "For the wages of sin is death" (6:23).

Sin brings death, a deserved punishment. God provided the Garden of Eden as a perfect environment for man. But Adam and Eve chose to rebel against God, and that was sin (Gen. 3:1-6). Since the person who sins will surely die, and we all have sinned, we all are condemned to spiritual, physical and eternal death (Rom. 5:12-21). What we need is someone to take away this penalty for our sin.

3. God's response

God knew all about our sin and need. He knew we needed a Savior, someone to appease His wrath for our sin. But that couldn't be just anyone; a perfect God could accept only a perfect sacrifice. God responded to our need with characteristic grace and love: "But God demonstrates His own love toward us, in that while we were still sinners, Christ died for us" (Rom. 5:8). Jesus was God's response to our need.

God provided His Son as Savior for us because we could not provide one for ourselves. "For He [God the Father] made Him [Jesus] who knew no sin to be sin for us, that we might become the righteousness of God in Him" (2 Cor. 5:21). God sent Jesus to die at

Calvary's cross to provide everything we need to be forgiven of our sin.

Jesus was God's response to our need.

---

4. Our reply

But salvation is not automatic. Romans 3:22 says "the righteousness of God . . . is through faith in Jesus Christ to all and on all who believe." God provided salvation through His Son, but to be saved we must believe that Jesus Christ is the only way for our sins to be forgiven. The key is the word *believe*. God's righteousness is on all who believe.

Our reply to God must be the reply of faith. "For by grace you have been saved through faith" (Eph. 2:8). If we believe Jesus died, was buried and raised from the dead specifically to save us from our sin, and we ask Him to save us, we will be saved (Acts 16:31). Without faith, it is impossible to please Him.

If you want your friends and family to know all they need to know to be saved, communicate to them these basics of God's program of salvation. Ask God to help you—He will.

What tools can you use?

If you really want to be a witness as a behind-the-lines missionary, what will you need? What are the missionary tools necessary to share your faith with your friends and neighbors? It may surprise you that you don't need a lot of big-ticket items to be a witness.

1. Use your Bible

I have led people to the Lord without a Bible in my hands, but it's much easier if they can see firsthand what God says about His love and their need. The basic tool for the behind-the-lines missionary is a Bible.

It's a good idea to mark the verses in your Bible you want to share with others. That way they can spot them easily. Underline or highlight them. Learn well where these verses are. Witnessing is not the time to be fumbling for the right book or chapter.

Share these basics with your friends. Pray before you meet with them; ask others to pray while you're meeting with your friends; and then pray with them after they choose to receive God's precious gift of salvation. That will help cement their decision.

2. Use literature and videos

There are other effective tools to help you tell your friends and family about the Lord. They aren't a substitute for the Bible, but they are an aid to take the Bible message to your friends.

Tracts have been a favorite and inexpensive way to share the Gospel. They are brief, easy-to-read and right to the point. Several fine tract societies print and distribute Gospel tracts.

In the last few years God has given us a new and very effective way of telling the Good News. Many times your friends will not attend church with you, but almost everyone will join you for an evening to watch a video. Back to the Bible has produced a number of Bible-teaching videos in its PASSPORT VIDEO series. Each of these videos was shot in the Holy Land or in other places significant in church history and features a presentation of the Gospel. After watching such a video, you can interact with your friends about what it means to trust Christ as Savior.

Books, booklets, Christian films and many other useful tools are also available to you. Check with your local Christian bookstore. But don't forget—a hammer is of no value to the carpenter until he uses it. When you purchase witnessing tools, be sure to use them.

3. Use your life

One of the easiest ways to share Christ is by the way you live. Allow the change in your life since you became a Christian to filter into every area of your life. Let your light shine in your neighborhood, on your job or at your family picnic in such a way that your friends and family see Jesus in your lifestyle.

Be joyful as a Christian. Be kind. Be forgiving. Be gentle. Be all Christ died to make you, and people will notice the difference. "Let your light so shine before men, that they may see your good works and glorify your Father in heaven" (Matt. 5:16).

Lifestyle evangelism alone is insufficient to lead people to the Savior. They need to know how to be saved, not just the lifestyle of the saved. But using your life as an evangelistic tool is a great way to be a behind-the-lines witness.

4. Use your head

The ways you can be a witness are as many and varied as there are Christians to be witnesses. Use your head. If you have an idea for witnessing that you think is good, check with your pastor or another mature Christian you trust. See what they think. There is safety in a multitude of counselors (Prov. 11:14; 24:6).

I have met people who used the mail as a witnessing tool. Others have used the telephone or the fax machine. Some have sponsored coffees and invited friends into the home so they could tell them about God's love. The possibilities are endless.

Behind-the-lines missionaries are not in a staging area. We are not just playing a support role. We are playing an active role in winning our world to Christ. Being a witness is not a "special somebody" thing; it's an "everybody" thing. If you have a story to tell, you can be a witness for the Lord.

Chapter 2

Be Active in Growing

Growth is the natural consequence of birth. Birth without growth is like a runner's starting blocks without a track—you have a place to start, but nowhere to go.

When you trust Jesus Christ as Savior, you are like a tiny pine seedling. You need to grow if you are to become strong and tall. If you don't grow in the grace and knowledge of our Lord and Savior Jesus Christ, you are apt to be snared by every new teaching that is spawned by every new fellowship group springing up in your community.

A major ingredient in success on the mission field is the continued personal growth of each servant of God. Even the most seasoned missionary needs daily growth in the Word.

But what about the behind-the-lines missionary? Is growth as necessary for us? Absolutely! Anyone who wants to bear fruit or be strong needs to grow, regardless of where they are called to serve.

The first century church was filled with missionaries, and they were very successful. Some of them went to Egypt, some went to Europe, and some stayed home. All were missionaries. What caused these behind-the-lines missionaries of Jerusalem to be as strong as their traveling counterparts? They all grew in the Lord.

We grow when we learn

When we speak of church growth, we naturally think of numerical growth. And why not? The early church grew dramatically in numbers.

Acts 2:41 says that "three thousand souls were added" to the church in one day. Acts 11:24 says that "a great many people were added to the Lord." But 5:14 is even more astounding: "And believers were increasingly added to the Lord, multitudes of both men and women." Words like *added* and *multitudes* tell the story. Numerical growth in the first century church was phenomenal.

But so was spiritual growth. These people started at square one—more so than people do today, for they had no historical knowledge of Christianity as we do. When spiritual newborns are properly taught, their rate of growth is astounding.

Acts 2:42 says, "And they continued steadfastly in the apostles' doctrine and fellowship, in the breaking of bread, and in prayers." The key to the rapid spiritual growth of these believers was their daily study in the Word.

If you are consistent in reading God's Word, if you study its truths alone or in a group, you can experience the kind of phenomenal growth these behind-the-lines missionaries in Jerusalem did. Here's how.

First, set a time each day to read and meditate on God's Word. Don't skip that time or let other things interfere. Keep a notebook handy to jot down things you learn from God's Word. Be taught by the greatest Teacher of all—the Holy Spirit. Grow by reading.

Second, attend a Bible-believing church consistently each week. Take notes from the pastor's sermons. If there isn't enough said worthy of taking notes, look for another church. There are plenty of God's servants worth listening to. Settle into a church where the Word is taught every week.

Spiritual growth comes from being taught God's Word.

Third, get involved in a Bible study group. Choose one that will do more than talk about problems. Choose one that will use God's Word to solve them. Remember, growth doesn't come from gab; it comes from being taught.

Fourth, listen to radio or television programs that teach the Word. Make sure the teachers are saying pretty much what your pastor says—if he is teaching the Word. Again, if you don't have something right out of the Bible to chew on after you have listened, you likely haven't learned from the Word.

Spiritual growth comes from being taught God's Word. It doesn't come from close calls or near misses at Bible study. It comes from daily, vibrant, consistent reading and thinking about what God says in the Bible.

We grow when we teach

Teaching may be the most powerful of all learning tools. When you study your Bible and share with your friends and family what you have learned, you do much more than teach. You learn again. You learn better. You learn deeper the truths you gleaned from your study of the Word.

Likely you've already experienced this. Perhaps you were asked to teach a Bible study group or a Sunday school class, so you prepared a lesson. You may have been scared to death when you taught, but you did your best. When your session was over, you discovered a valuable truth: The teacher always learns more than the student.

If you want to grow in the Lord, learn from His Word and then teach what you have learned to others. You'll see your growth deepen and broaden at the same time.

Apollos was a first century Christian who was eloquent in the Scriptures. He was skillful in speaking and teaching others the Word of God. But his knowledge was not complete; he knew only of the water baptism of John. He knew nothing of the baptism of the Spirit of which Jesus spoke.

Enter Priscilla and Aquila. This godly couple were students of the Word. Daily they studied the Scriptures. When Apollos came to Ephesus, they took him aside and instructed him more accurately in the Word (Acts 18:24–26). In teaching him, they were learning for themselves. It always works that way. Teachers are the best learners, so to learn more of the Bible, take every opportunity to teach it to others.

We grow when we serve

There's no teacher like experience. The more you learn, the more you teach. The more you teach, the more you serve. The more you serve, the more you learn.

Behind-the-lines missionaries experience different things from front-line missionaries, but we gain experience nonetheless. The more we serve the Lord with what we have learned from His Word, the more we learn from His Word. That's not a vicious cycle—it's a victorious cycle.

Paul visited Ephesus on many occasions. Acts 18:11 says that he continued there a year and a half, "teaching the word of God among them." He also reminded the Ephesian elders that he served the Lord with humility (20:19). For Paul, teaching and serving were the same thing. He served by teaching. He learned by teaching. He grew by teaching.

Behind-the-lines missionaries need to grow, and we grow the same way front-line missionaries grow. You don't have to be a professional missionary like Paul to grow in the Lord. Just do what he did. Learn the Word, teach what you have learned, and serve the Lord in the way He enables you.

Be active in growing spiritually strong. After all, it does an army little good to grow strong front-line soldiers if the supply-line soldiers are weak and stunted in growth. Regardless of who you are or how you serve, be consistently growing in your knowledge of God's Word. That's what keeps God's army battle-ready.

Chapter 3

Be Active in Serving

Have you ever heard the expression "Bloom where you are planted"? That's appropriate advice for behind-the-lines missionaries. God has a work for each of us to do, where He has planted us to do it. Another way of saying the same thing is "Serve where you are saved."

When the church at Jerusalem began to grow rapidly, thousands being added at a time, problems arose. The church had to address these problems without the benefit of experience or a policies and procedures manual.

One of these issues is recorded in Acts 6. Many of the wealthier believers had sold their property to aid the poorer believers, but some of the Greek-speaking Jews felt the needs of their widows were not being adequately cared for. So the disciples arranged for seven men to serve as deacons—those who administered the church's charitable allocations.

These men were not preachers, apostles, teachers, itinerant evangelists, traveling missionaries or any of the other "glamorous" ministries. They were table servers, keepers of the home fires. They were people just like you and me. They were the behind-the-lines missionaries, and they were important to God and His church. Their attitudes toward serving as a genuine ministry are guidelines for us today. Let's examine their attitudes.

Service is a calling of God

Someone has said that service is the rent we pay for the space we occupy in this world. But as Christians, we should be more interested in the space we occupy in the Body of Christ than in the world.

Do you see serving the Lord as a divine calling? If you're saved, it is. To be free from the bondage of Satan and sin does not mean you and I are free to do whatever we want. We are simply free to serve God as He wants, and that's real freedom.

When Moses stood before Pharaoh and said, "Let My people go," he gave a reason each time he made that demand. He didn't just say, "Let My people go"; he told Pharaoh why God's people were to be freed. "Let My people go, that they may serve Me in the wilderness" (Ex. 7:16; cf. 4:23; 8:1, 20; 9:1, 13; 10:3, 7).

God didn't save the Israelites because He felt sorry for them. He saved them so they could serve Him, and that's true of you and me as well.

We should never read or quote Ephesians 2:8–9 without verse 10. That's the verse that tells us why God saved us: "For we are His workmanship, created [saved] in Christ Jesus for good works, which God prepared beforehand that we should walk in them."

Each of us must see our salvation as God's call to us to serve Him. These Jerusalem deacons were happy to serve tables for the Lord; that was their calling of God. That's what gave meaning to their Christian life.

If once we are saved we're on our way to heaven, why doesn't God just take us home? If it's so much better there, why does He leave us here? Because He has something for us to do. One day, when the battle is over, all of our opportunity for earthly service will be over as well. We must see ourselves as called of God to serve now, or we will miss this opportunity forever.

Service is a high calling of God

Don't think that if you aren't called to go to the other side of the world in service that your calling isn't important. It isn't your calling anyway; it's God's calling. You are the one called.

Servants of the Lord have always been prompted to see their service as a very high calling. The Levites served the tabernacle and temple of God in the Old Testament, much like the deacons served the church in the New Testament. Levites gave up their land and their identity in this world in exchange for the privilege of the high calling of God (Num. 18:21).

Behind-the-lines servants are not second-class servants.

And what was this high calling? What duties did they perform?

They served as assistants to the priests in the worship system of Israel. They took care of the tabernacle and the temple and performed other menial duties

(Num. 8:6–19). Today they would be the janitors of the church. They saw this as their calling, a high calling because it was from God.

We should see our service to the Lord the same way. It's not always the talented people who serve the Lord best—it's the most consecrated ones. Behind-the-lines servants are not second-class servants. But they are obedient servants, serving God where they are called to serve Him.

Service is a personal calling of God

If God doesn't call you to be a Bible translator, a church planter or a preaching missionary, don't worry. He has called you to do something else for Him. Find out what it is and then do it. Your calling is a personal calling. You can't do successfully what God has not called you to do, but He will enable you to do whatever He has called you to do.

S. S. Kresge, the founder of Kresge's Department Stores (now Kmart), said, "Find out where you can render a service; then render it. The rest is up to the Lord." He's so right.

God is a personal God. He shapes and moulds our calling just as He shapes and moulds us. He has a service with your name on it. He is calling you today to do something special for Him, and it may be right there in your church.

What has He put in your hand? That's where you begin to serve the Lord. That's how He has moulded you. That's what He has for you to do until He changes your calling.

Remember Dorcas? She was a woman full of good works and charitable deeds (Acts 9:36). That was her behind-the-lines calling. She didn't preach—she sewed.

Dorcas was a great missionary. Why? Because she did what God called her to do. Obedience, consecration, faithfulness—these are qualities God is looking for in His servants—not necessarily visas, passports and prayer cards.

Your mission field may be in the church nursery. Don't miss God's calling by constantly looking at "whiter" fields. Serve where you are saved. If God wants you to serve Him elsewhere, He'll make that known to you. In the meantime, consider what you are doing for God as the highest calling possible. It is.

Chapter 4

Be Active in Seasoning

In the last two decades, we have come to realize in greater measure just how much the world needs seasoning.

I was born in the 1940s and remember fondly the innocence of my youth. The 1950s was perhaps the most carefree decade in modern history. I spent my boyhood in that decade.

We began each day in school by reading the Bible, saying the Pledge of Allegiance to the American flag and praying to God. Life was considered extremely precious in those days—the Hippocratic oath was upheld. Doctors were battling polio, and Jonas Salk became a hero when he developed a vaccine for it.

How things have changed in my lifetime. Instead of preserving life, some doctors have discovered a lucrative gold mine in killing children in the womb. Kids aren't taking Bibles to school anymore; now they're taking guns. Metal detectors used to be a novelty; now they are as common as an exit door.

It's no secret that violent crime, drive-by shootings, aggravated assault and rape have skyrocketed in the last few decades. Our society is disintegrating before our eyes. We act more like animals than animals do. Only a fool thinks that increased technology, increased leisure and increased education have done anything but produce well-educated, high-tech thugs with time on their hands.

Perhaps it's time we reevaluated one aspect of Christ's call to His followers. Maybe we should see the seasoning of our society as a missionary calling, just as much as taking the message to a pagan society. After all, most pagan societies aren't as pagan as we Westerners have become.

The first century church was engaged in a seasoning ministry, a call to be salt and light in their community. The Jerusalem Christians were hauled into court and commanded not to teach in the name of Jesus. Instead, they filled the city with the story of salvation in Jesus' name. When reprimanded, Peter said, "We ought to obey God rather than men" (Acts 5:29).

Some of you may be called to be behind-the-lines missionaries as seasoners. Let's see how Christ calls us to a ministry of seasoning.

Matthew 5 contains Jesus' Beatitudes. These blessings are pronounced on people who possess various attitudes, such as meekness or a thirst for righteousness. They conclude with a blessing on those who are persecuted and falsely perjured for the sake of Christ. That sets the tone for what Jesus next teaches us— that we have a specific calling as behind-the-lines missionaries.

Called to be salt

"You are the salt of the earth," Jesus said. (Matt. 5:13). On the surface, that seems like a strange thing to say to faithful disciples.

In the ancient Near East, salt was used in a variety of ways. Its characteristics—pungency, flavor, preservative power—made it a striking metaphor.

It's likely that this last quality—the potency of salt as a preservative, even an antiseptic—is what Jesus had in mind when He told His disciples to be the salt of the earth. As an antiseptic preservative, salt retards decay and keeps food from spoiling. It maintains all the beneficial qualities while keeping in check the harmful qualities. In this respect, salt has a negative function. It combats deterioration.

Behind-the-lines missionaries are saline missionaries.

In this same way, God calls us to combat the deterioration of our society. That's as much a ministry as building up society, but it's far less likely to be appreciated.

Our society needs more salt. Front-line missionaries are sailing missionaries; behind-the-lines missionaries are saline missionaries. Maybe you're called to be active in the war against moral disintegration in your home country. If so, your call is to be active in seasoning your society rather than evangelizing another.

If the missionary enterprise around the world is to be healthy, the countries that have been missionary launching pads must be equally healthy. Presently, the United States, Canada, Great Britain and other nations that have been great sending nations are so morally bankrupt they have become mission fields instead.

If God has called you to a ministry of writing letters to your congressman or protesting a porn shop in your neighborhood, don't be hesitant. That's being salt. If God has impressed you to become part of the anti-abortion movement, see your participation as being seasoning to a rotting world. You may be a behind-the-lines missionary, but when the lines are drawn, you could be surprised how close you are to the front.

Called to be light

Immediately after calling His disciples to a ministry as salt, Jesus calls them to a ministry of light. "You are the light of the world" (v. 14). As salt has a negative function, light has a positive function.

Salt preserves society so light can shine in it without hindrance. Both are necessary. Nobody is saved by salt alone, but a society that won't tolerate salt won't turn to the light. Behind-the-lines missionaries must be both.

In the Bible, light indicates the true knowledge of God (Matt. 6:22–23). It symbolizes the best in learning. When your friends and neighbors turn to Jesus, a light is turned on in their life. Light and life go together (John 1:4). When you let the light of Jesus Christ shine in your life, your friends see the Light, Jesus Christ.

Jesus said we should not put a basket over our light (Matt. 5:15–16), that we should not do things as missionaries that dim our witness behind the lines.

When we do, we not only dim our light, we weaken the effect of our seasoning as well. We become part of the problem rather than part of the solution.

Ask God what kind of ministry He has for you. Perhaps it's taking an active part in seasoning your society to strengthen it for the missionary enterprise around the world. Your participation on a local school board may open the door for the Light to shine again in public education. Taking part in a life chain may communicate to your government that there's something rotten in this world (abortion) and you want to bring your salt to bear on it.

Behind-the-lines missionaries are just as important as front-line missionaries, and the front keeps coming closer to our door. If we aren't active in a ministry of seasoning and evangelism, we may discover the enemy at our door.

Don't be a spiritual couch potato. Be salt and light in a nation that needs both your negative and positive ministry. Be a missionary to your society.

Chapter 5

Be Active in Praying

There are some activities associated with people not called to cross the seas, learn a new language and translate the Bible into that language. The ministry of prayer is one of them. That's why missionaries always say, "Pray for us." That's why their pictures are on prayer cards, not post cards. Prayer is an expected behind-the-lines ministry.

It's also hard work. Because we don't frequently see the faces of those who have asked us to pray for them, prayer is too often a neglected work.

Have you been called to a ministry of prayer? All Christians are called to pray, right? Prayer is one of the great privileges of the believer. It was purchased for us by the blood of Jesus Christ. But my question still stands. Have you been called to a ministry of prayer?

To gain some insight into this behind-the-lines ministry, let's look at the prayer life of the early church. Prayer in the first century was held in high esteem. Let's see why.

Prayer was consistent

Do you know how far into the Book of Acts you have to read before you encounter the church praying? Not far at all. Acts 1:14 records the first of many times prayer is highlighted in this book.

The disciples had returned to the upper room from the Mount of Olives just after Jesus' ascension into heaven. They gathered together in one accord, in a mutual spirit. What do believers do when they are one in spirit? They pray. "These all continued with one accord in prayer and supplication" (v. 14).

The early church needed some glue to hold itself together. They could witness separately. They could preach singly. But they prayed together.

Their public prayer matched their private prayer. Acts 3:1 says, "Peter and John went up together to the temple at the hour of prayer, the ninth hour." Imagine. Impetuous, intrepid Peter and timid, tenuous John—perhaps our Lord's most diverse disciple—went together to the temple to pray. They were consistent in praying at the ninth hour, and likely at the other designated hours for temple prayers.

Do you have a ministry of prayer? We all pray—at meal time, when we're in trouble, when we go to bed—but if you have a ministry of prayer, you pray consistently, at specified times, for specific requests.

Prayer was urgent

Suppose missionaries your church supports are planning to return to the field soon. Everything is in order except one thing—they haven't received their visas to return. Time is drawing short. They need significant prayer. Whom do they call first?

Does your face come to their minds? It likely does if you have been given the ministry of prayer. When the need for prayer is urgent, we want to know whom to call.

Frequently in the life of the early church, prayer was urgent. When Herod brutally killed James the brother of John, fear gripped the Jerusalem Christians (Acts 12:1–2). Who would be next?

Soon Peter was picked up by the Roman soldiers and thrown into prison. But the church knew what to do. Verse 5 says, "Constant prayer was offered to God for him by the church." Apparently, quite a number of the Jerusalem church were behind-the-lines missionaries engaged in a ministry of prayer. And it worked.

God sent an angel to Peter and led him out of the prison to the Jerusalem street. The apostle headed straight for the house of Mary, the mother of John Mark (v. 12). Do you know why? Because that's where people had gathered to pray. How did Peter know they would be gathered there? That's where they always gathered. Mary was a behind-the-lines missionary given a ministry of prayer.

Do you have a ministry of prayer? You do if you believe God has called you to it and you're one of the first people others call to pray. When the need is urgent, your ministry of prayer becomes even more urgent.

Prayer was important

How important is prayer to you? Alfred, Lord Tennyson said, "More things are wrought by prayer than this world dreams of." He's so right. Prayer was incredibly important to the early church. They saw it as their chief source of power.

Remember when the Greek-speaking Jews were concerned about their widows being neglected? The disciples appointed seven men of good reputation, full of the Holy Spirit and wisdom to care for these widows. And what did the Twelve do? They said, "We will give ourselves continually to prayer and to the ministry of the word" (Acts 6:4).

Notice the position given to prayer. It was awarded the same status as the ministry of the Word. To the disciples, the ministry of prayer equalled in importance the ministry of the Word.

Have you heard the expression "If you can't give and you can't go, you can always pray"? That saying makes it sound as if Christians have established a rating system for ministry importance. It's like scoring at the Olympics. Going to a foreign field is worth a 5.8 score. Giving money is at least a 5.6. But praying for those on the field is only a 3.5.

The ministry of prayer equalled in importance the ministry of the Word.

If God has called you to be a behind-the-lines missionary active in prayer, you should never feel like a second-class Christian. The ministry of prayer was held in high esteem by the early church. It should be held in high esteem by us too.

The most important ministry is the one God calls you to. If He has called you to a ministry of prayer, don't ever think your ministry is unimportant.

Without behind-the-lines missionaries like you, there would be no victories on the front line.

Chapter 6

Be Active in Sending

One of the major ministries of those who are called to remain behind is the ministry of sending out those who are called to go. It's a genuine privilege to participate in a church commissioning service in which a missionary is sent to the mission field.

If you are a member of a local church that believes the Bible and is active in winning people to Christ, challenging them in the Word and sending them into the world, you can be a behind-the-scenes participant in one of the most fulfilling of all ministries—the sending ministry.

Let's go back to our first century Christian friends to see how it works.

The church exercised its authority

The first missionaries were sent out not from the Jerusalem church but from the church at Antioch. Acts 13:1–3 records this event.

> *Now in the church that was at Antioch there were certain prophets and teachers: Barnabas, Simeon who was called Niger, Lucius of Cyrene, Manaen who had been brought up with Herod the tetrarch, and Saul. As they ministered to the Lord and fasted, the Holy Spirit said, 'Now separate to*

*Me Barnabas and Saul for the work to which I
have called them.' Then, having fasted and prayed,
and laid hands on them, they sent them away.*

The authority to send missionaries to foreign lands was placed in the hands of the church. Who made up the church at Antioch? People just like you and me.

God has placed the authority to commission His ambassadors to the world in the hands of Christians who are members of their local assembly. Mission boards help churches send missionaries. They are facilitators, but only your church has the biblical authority to be the sender. If you are a member of a church, you are empowered corporately with this great privilege. As a behind-the-lines missionary, you have the joy of sending to the field front-line missionaries.

The candidate proved his authenticity

But whom will you send? Who in your congregation is the man or woman God would have you commission as a front-line missionary? Let's see how it was done in the early church.

Acts 13:1–3 indicates that it was within the context of service in the local church that men were identified as prophets and teachers. All the qualities of a good missionary—integrity, honesty, faithfulness, evangelistic zeal, godliness—have to be demonstrated by servants at home before those servants can be dedicated to service abroad.

That's how Timothy was selected for missionary service. Paul led Timothy to the Lord on his first missionary journey. Then he returned to Timothy's hometown looking for a traveling companion. Notice how the selection process took place:

> *Then he came to Derbe and Lystra. And behold, a certain disciple was there, named Timothy, the son of a certain Jewish woman who believed, but his father was Greek. He was well spoken of by the brethren who were at Lystra and Iconium. Paul wanted to have him go on with him.* (Acts 16:1–3)

The sincerity, service and sacrificial attitude of Timothy were authenticated by the members of the church at Lystra. He was well thought of by the other Christians there. He had all the right qualities. So the church said to Paul, "Timothy's your man. Take him."

The early church was constantly grooming its young people to become leaders at home and "sent ones" to the field.

The early church was constantly grooming its young people to become leaders at home and "sent ones" to the field. Is your church doing that today? When was the last time you had the joy as a behind-the-lines missionary of sending out a front-line missionary?

Don't let the finest, the brightest, the sharpest young people of your church be recruited by science

41

and industry when they could be recruited for full-time service for the Lord. What higher calling could they have?

The Holy Spirit gave His approval

We don't just pick any Tom, Dick or Harry out of the youth group and send them to a far-off land. We must seek the approval of the Holy Spirit for every missionary candidate. That's where you come in as well.

Did you notice in Acts 13 that prayer and fasting accompanied both the seeking process and the sending process? The believers prayed and fasted before they decided which of the believers should travel to the field. And they prayed and fasted when they commissioned them to go.

You and I, the ordinary members of the local church, should do the same. We behind-the-lines missionaries have a ministry of sending front-line missionaries to the field.

You may not be called to go overseas; not everyone is. You may not be gifted to preach; not everyone is. You may not be capable of giving to keep a missionary on the field; not everyone is. But we are the Church, and we do have the authority to be God's sending agency for world missions. That authority translates into constant recruitment from the ranks of our congregation and constant prayer and fasting in order to discern God's will.

If you're a member of a local church, then you have a role to play in the sending process that is just as important as the role played by those called to go.

Reflect on what God has called you to do today, and then be faithful in doing it.

Chapter 7
Be Active in Facilitating

So you're not called to board a jet and fly to a remote corner of the world to serve the Lord. Does that mean you are excluded from the great task of taking the Gospel around the world? Not in the least. One of the greatest ways you can be a behind-the-lines missionary is to be a facilitator.

A facilitator is someone who makes things easier. The cause of Christ needs such facilitators at home—people who will help make the missionary's efforts easier. There are many ways you can be a facilitator without being a pastor or missions committee member.

Provide orientation

Perhaps the most difficult time in the Christian life are those first few months after you are saved and you begin attending church. New converts in the first century knew little or nothing about Jesus, and that's true today as well. New believers need someone to befriend them, to facilitate their orientation into the church. Ananias was such a facilitator.

In Acts 9, the greatest persecutor of the church in the first century was gloriously saved. On the road to Damascus, Saul of Tarsus encountered the Lord Jesus, and his life was changed forever. But who of the church at Damascus knew what happened to Paul? No one.

So God chose Ananias to facilitate bringing the great persecutor into the church. At first Ananias was understandably afraid of Saul (v.13), but soon he referred to this new convert as "Brother Saul" (v. 17).

Are there people who have just come to Christ who are having a hard time acclimating to your church? Maybe they have had a very godless background. Maybe they are a bit shabby and tattered around the edges. You can be a special behind-the-scenes missionary to them by sitting with them in church, helping them find a Sunday school class or inviting them to your home Bible study group.

When a new Christian begins attending your church, don't criticize his appearance or lack of "Christian couth." Instead, see him as a potential giant for Christ. When Chuck Colson, President Richard Nixon's "hatchet man," received Christ as his Savior while in prison, someone had to ease his entry into the church. Maybe it's what God has in mind for you.

Provide physical care

Paul and Silas were beaten and thrown into prison at Philippi. There they prayed and sang praises at midnight. That you knew, but did you know that after the Philippian jailer and his family trusted Christ as Savior, they immediately became facilitators of the Gospel?

Acts 16:33 says, "And he took them the same hour of the night and washed their stripes." This man was a jailer, not a doctor. But he facilitated the spread of the Gospel by tending to the physical needs of two missionaries.

A facilitator is someone who makes things easier.

A few years ago I was preaching in Canada and had a horrible cold. I needed to see a doctor and get some antibiotics, but it was Sunday. The pastor invited me to have lunch with his family. His son was visiting from a distant city in Canada. At the table I discovered the son was a physician and had some antibiotics with him, which he gladly administered to me. He helped me on my way. He facilitated the preaching of the Gospel message by tending to my physical needs.

One of the greatest needs for missionaries on furlough is rest. Do you have a time-share condominium or an apartment somewhere? Why not facilitate the missionaries' "R & R" by letting them use your time-share for a week? Or what about paying their way to a Bible conference for a week? They'll be refreshed both physically and spiritually.

There is always something we can do to facilitate spreading the Gospel if we look for opportunities.

Provide a meeting place

Most churches don't begin with a building. They begin with a Bible study group in someone's home. If there is a need for a Bible-believing church in your town or in your part of town, why not be a facilitator of the Gospel by opening your home to be the meeting place for a new church?

Justus did that in ancient Corinth. Acts 18 records that Paul planted the church in Corinth by preaching each Sabbath in the Corinthian synagogue. But soon there was opposition, and the fledgling church needed a place to meet.

Verse 7 says, "And he departed from there and entered the house of a certain man named Justus, one who worshiped God, whose house was next door to the synagogue." There the church was established and continued for a year and a half (v. 11).

Perhaps you are called to facilitate the preaching of the Gospel by opening your home for a new church or a Five-day Club or Backyard Club for children. Make your house or your yard a temple for God. Consecrate it for Him, and take an active part in spreading the Gospel.

Provide travel services

Acts 17:10 says, "Then the brethren immediately sent Paul and Silas away by night to Berea." The Christians at Thessalonica provided travel services to escort Paul to Berea—and that in the middle of the night! Then the Berean believers escorted Paul from their village all the way to Athens (v. 15).

How far is it to Berea from Thessalonica? I've traveled that road, and it's about 45 miles of rugged terrain. But that's nothing compared with the distance from Berea to Athens. That's nearly 300 miles. Of course, the Christians may have sailed with Paul to Athens, but that doesn't make their effort any less dramatic.

These brethren accompanied Paul all the way to Athens, and then they returned immediately to Berea to tell Silas and Timothy to join Paul in Athens.

What were the names of these brethren? Were they called to be apostles? No. Were they called to preach? No. Were they called to write books on theology? No. Who were they? They were facilitators, people who made the spread of the Gospel easier. They were very important to Paul, and they were very important to God.

I fly to almost every conference at which I preach. Someone must pick me up at the airport and return me to the airport after the conference is over. Those who facilitate my getting to and from where I preach are the modern equivalent of the brethren in Berea. Those who drive me to the meetings or to pray with people who have a specific need are facilitators of the ministry. They are as important to God as I am because both of us are necessary for the spread of the Gospel.

Are you a facilitator? You could be if you let God use you in any of the ways mentioned here. And there are many more ways. Being a behind-the-lines missionary is a great privilege. Enjoy that privilege as a facilitator of the Gospel.

Chapter 8

Be Active in Financing

Any discussion of missions eventually comes to our role in giving money so that the Gospel can be preached around the world. It's usually here that we begin to fidget and squirm and hope that the topic will soon change. That's a shame, because we've finally come to something that almost every one of us can do as behind-the-lines missionaries.

Behind-the-lines missionaries who finance the spread of the Gospel are the most critically needed people in the world today. Tragically, those who are called and trained can't find enough financing to get to the field. They end up doing something other than what God has called them to do, and it's not their fault. Their failure is the failure of behind-the-lines missionaries to do our part.

Today the greatest hindrance to the spread of the Gospel isn't closed doors or language barriers. It's the perceived need to have all those things that make us the typical consumer, consuming more and more that's irrelevant to eternity while consecrating less and less that isn't.

Compare our present attitudes toward giving with those of the early church. Ask yourself if your giving patterns to missions are all the Lord Jesus expects.

Giving was a necessity

The first century church did not finance the spread of Christianity only when they received a heart-rending appeal letter or saw the sad face of a starving child. Behind-the-lines giving was consistent because it was necessary, just as necessary as going to the front lines. They saw it as no less important.

As early as Acts 2 we see the giving patterns of the early church. "Now all who believed were together, and had all things in common, and sold their possessions and goods, and divided them among all, as anyone had need" (vv. 44–45).

Not long ago I received a letter from a couple who were former students of mine. They both felt the call to missions. After they completed their education and were married, they went to missionary candidate school and then hit the road on pre-field ministry.

This couple had everything going for them. They were both bright, attractive, godly people—one of the sharpest couples I have ever known. They represented the Lord capably. But their letter said that after more than three years of deputation and hardly enough financial commitments to make a dent in their needs, their mission agency was asking them to change to a field in which less financing was necessary.

What happened? Insufficient behind-the-lines support. Too few people saw the necessity of making a financial sacrifice so this couple could impact the world as front-line missionaries. If that had been true of the Jerusalem church, you and I wouldn't have the Gospel today.

Giving was a privilege

The early church saw giving as more than a necessity. They saw it as a privilege as well.

"All who were possessors of lands or houses sold them, and brought the proceeds of the things that were sold, and laid them at the apostles' feet" (4:34–35). The early Christians were, by in large, very poor people. It was not the wealthy of society but the poor who followed Christ. They were common people, slaves, blue-collar workers. The church couldn't count on many $100,000 gifts; they were more accustomed to $10 gifts.

But they all understood the principle that to whom much is given, much is required (Luke 12:48). Giving was a privilege because the believers were privileged to have something to sell in order to give. Not everyone did, of course, but those who did thanked God for His blessing and didn't hesitate to trade in that temporal blessing for eternal reward.

One such behind-the-lines missionary was Barnabas, a Levite who hailed from the island of Cyprus. There he owned some property, probably a family inheritance. He was one of the privileged to have wealth, but he saw it as a privilege to sell his land in order to finance the needs of the church (Acts 4:36–37).

Contrast Barnabas' attitude with the prevailing attitude of many Christians today. They say they've worked hard for what they have, and it belongs to them. Apparently many people have forgotten Ecclesiastes 5:19: "As for every man to whom God has given riches and wealth, and given him power to eat of it, to receive his heritage and rejoice in his labor—this is the gift of God."

When we see all that we possess as a gift from God, we'll have less difficulty financing the front-line missionary. We'll see giving as a privilege, because we're privileged to have something to give.

Giving was a sacrifice

The more we have, the more we can give. But if we have a lot, giving a lot is not necessarily a sacrifice. That's why, like David, the Jerusalem church believed they should not offer to the Lord God that which cost them nothing (2 Sam. 24:24). Those who had more, gave more, until their sacrifice equalled that of those who had little to give. Again, Barnabas is a case in point.

He sold his land to give to the Lord God, and He gave all that he received from the sale. It was the greatest financial sacrifice possible. Contrast that with Ananias and Sapphira a few verses later (Acts 5:1-3). They, too, sold land they possessed, but they held back part of the profit from the sale. Their sacrifice was less, even though they attempted to fool the church into thinking it was more.

Only God knows the extent of your financial sacrifice as a behind-the-lines missionary. When you give sacrificially, you need not tell anyone about it; God knows. But when you fail to give sacrificially, God knows that too.

Giving was a gateway

One final observation about the giving of Barnabas as a behind-the-lines missionary: Financing the needs

54

of the church was a gateway to additional service for Barnabas.

This man is mentioned 24 times in the Book of Acts. He comes on the scene as a donor; he ends up as a "sent one," a missionary in the strictest sense of the word. When we are faithful in one calling, sometimes God calls us to faithfulness in another.

Giving is the entry-level service to God.

Barnabas saw financing the mission of the church as a calling. He had the ability to give, the church had a need, and God called him to fill that need. But sometimes our response to financial need is the prerequisite to other forms of service. That was true with Barnabas. Maybe it's true of you too.

In Acts 13, Barnabas was one of the prophets and teachers in the church at Antioch. The Holy Spirit said, "Now separate to Me Barnabas and Saul for the work to which I have called them" (v. 2). Changed circumstances meant a changed call. Faithfulness in one calling fostered trust in another calling.

Giving is the entry-level service to God. That's something we all can do to some extent. Who knows what God has in store for you if you faithfully respond to His claim on your finances?

The privilege of front-line missionaries is to stand toe-to-toe with the devil and fight for the souls of men and women. The privilege of behind-the-lines missionaries is to stand toe-to-toe with the devil and fight for the finances necessary to keep men and women on the front lines. Exercise your privilege with cheerfulness.

Chapter 9

Be Active in Entertaining

Have you ever heard someone say, "She's the perfect hostess"? Perhaps that has been said about you. Someone appreciated your kindness in preparing a room or a meal for him. This is one of the nicest ways for you to be a behind-the-lines missionary.

The Bible is filled with examples of perfect hosts and hostesses. They grace the sacred pages throughout every age of history. But where are they today? Where are the perfect hosts and hostesses in Christian circles today? Most of them belong to the McDonald's family or the Ramada family.

The lost art of being a blessing

The Greek word for hospitality literally means "love of strangers." We begin to understand the love of strangers when Abraham entertained angels, unaware of who they were. He invited them into his house, washed their feet, prepared fresh meat and had Sarah bake fresh bread for them (Gen. 18:1–8).

Even today the traditional greeting to guests at a Bedouin tent in the Middle East is "You are among your family."

Such hospitality was commanded by God. Leviticus 19:33–34 says, "And if a stranger sojourns with you in your land, you shall not mistreat him. But the stranger who dwells among you shall be to you as one born among you, and you shall love him as yourself."

Eating a meal or spending the night were the two basics of Middle Eastern hospitality. How often Jesus ate and lodged at the homes of His acquaintances—whether old friends like Lazarus, Mary and Martha (John 12:1–2) or new friends like Zacchaeus (Luke 19:5-7).

The Book of Acts reflects the hospitality of the early church. Paul was entertained in the homes of Lydia (Acts 16:14–15), the Philippian jailer (vv. 32–34), Priscilla and Aquila (18:3), Philip (21:8), Mnason (v. 16) and Publius (28:7).

So you're not called to cross the ocean and translate the Bible into a foreign tongue. You can be a behind-the-lines missionary by entertaining some of those who have crossed the ocean. In this way you will be a blessing to others.

The pathway to receiving a blessing

But there's more to the ministry of entertaining than being a blessing. There's also receiving a blessing.

A most frightening thing happened to Paul while sailing to Rome as a prisoner of the Roman government (Acts 27–28). A horrible storm arose, and Paul's ship broke apart and sank. Fortunately, the island of Malta was nearby, and all passengers were able to swim to shore.

On the island Paul was entertained at the estate of Malta's leading citizen—a man named Publius. Paul stayed there three days and discovered that his host's father was sick with dysentery. He prayed for the man, laid hands on him and healed him. If hospitality had not been offered, healing would not have occurred. We receive a blessing when we are a blessing.

But physical blessings are not the only kind. Spiritual blessings also come as a result of the ministry of entertainment.

We receive a blessing when we are a blessing.

My father was a pastor. I don't have enough fingers and toes to count the times I gave up my bed as a boy for a visiting missionary, evangelist or chalk artist. Yet I never complained. I had the unique spiritual blessing of sitting at the table and hearing stories of how God was working in people's lives all over the world.

More than anything else, those occasions formed my thirst to take the Gospel to the world. It was a spiritual clinic for me as a young boy. It was like going to school without paying tuition.

The next time your pastor is looking for someone to prepare a bag lunch for the visiting youth group or provide a room for a Christian couple from a distant city, think about being a behind-the-lines missionary. If you have the ministry of hospitality, you have the ministry of missions. Be a blessing and be blessed.

The basics of providing a blessing

Perhaps your children are now grown and gone. You have some extra room in your home and you'd like to use it for the Lord as a ministry of entertainment. How do you go about it?

Remember the story of Elisha and the Shunammite woman? She noticed the regularity of his travels and convinced her husband to build a little prophet's chamber for Elisha, a place where he could rest when he was in the village (2 Kings 4:10).

If you are thinking of turning a spare room into a prophet's chamber for visiting evangelists, Bible teachers, drama teams, etc., here are some guidelines for you.

1. Size is not important; cleanliness is. The room the Shunammite couple made for Elisha was not gigantic. However, it would be hard to imagine that this notable woman would not have a spotless house. Make sure your prophet's chamber is well dusted, the linen freshly washed and the room adequately ventilated.

2. Privacy is important. The Shunammite's room was an upper room on the outside wall of the house at the roof level. It likely had a private entrance. I once remember spending the night with a German Shepherd on my bed. The pastor in whose house I was staying thought he had given me a private room because his daughters had vacated it. But the dog knew better. Give your visiting prophet privacy.

3. Furnishings don't have to be fancy. In Elisha's chamber there was just a bed, a table and a chair with a lampstand—not very elaborate, but functional. Your

guests come to rest; the bed is the most important piece of furniture for them. If you're going to be a good entertainer, don't put your worst mattress on the prophet's bed. He may look more like a pretzel than a prophet in the morning.

4. Give the opportunity for social interaction with your family, but don't demand it. Perhaps your guest has messages to prepare or papers to grade or something else that demands quiet solitude. Second Kings 4:10 says that the Shunammite couple made a room for Elisha so "whenever he comes to us, he can turn in there." It doesn't say anything about a gab session until midnight. Elisha turned into the house as often as he wanted and apparently turned into bed whenever he wanted.

5. A good hostess respects the wishes of her guests. If your prophet stays for a meal and asks for lunch to be light, he probably means it. Once while speaking at a church, I knew I was to have a banquet lunch at 1:00 p.m., so I asked my hostess to go easy on me for dinner. She agreed. I showed up at her home for a 5:00 meal of roast turkey, dressing, potatoes, three kinds of vegetables and on and on. She wanted to be the perfect hostess, but she wasn't.

See what God has put into your hand as a tool for ministry—even if it's a sauce pan or a pillow case. There are too many examples of the ministry of hospitality in the Bible to be coincidental. Perhaps this is the ministry God has in mind for you. If so, cherish it, enjoy it, be faithful to it. All the Elishas—young and old—who come by your chamber will thank God for you.

Chapter 10

Be Active in Encouraging

Encouragement is defined as "the act of inspiring with courage, spirit or hope." It means to give help or patronage to someone. In missions, sometimes encouragement is the best thing you can give. All of us occasionally need this ministry.

Someone said that a friend will strengthen you with his prayers, bless you with his love and encourage you with his hope. Front-line missionaries need friends who will pray for them. They need friends who will love them. And they need friends who will encourage them with hope.

Barnabas was an encourager. In fact, his name means "Son of Encouragement." He knew the value of being a friend.

Barnabas encouraged his fellow believers with gifts of financial help (Acts 4:36–37). Financial support is a sure way to encourage missionaries. But there are many other ways the early Christians encouraged one another.

Front-line missionaries need encouragement like everybody else. Behind-the-lines missionaries are in the perfect position to provide that encouragement. Let's see how.

Send them on their way

If you have never left home knowing that you would not return for months or years, you can't appreciate what missionaries feel when leaving home for the first time. You can have a significant behind-the-lines ministry by being there when missionaries embark on their front-line ministry. Just be there. Show them you care.

Paul spent more time as a missionary in Ephesus than in any other city. His departure from there was a tender moment. Acts 20:36–38 says, "And when he had said these things, he knelt down and prayed with them all. Then they all wept freely, and fell on Paul's neck and kissed him, sorrowing most of all for the words which he spoke, that they would see his face no more. And they accompanied him to the ship."

Those Ephesians knew how to give a send-off. It was genuine, emotional and something Paul would never forget. You can give your front-line missionaries that same kind of send-off. Pray with them. Hug them. Be there for them.

Greet them on arrival back home

Equal in importance to a sincere send-off is a genuine welcome home. Acts 21:17 says, "And when we had come to Jerusalem, the brethren received us gladly." Jerusalem wasn't home for Paul, but it seemed like it. He spent much time in Jerusalem before he was saved and with the Jerusalem church afterward.

When you call a new pastor to your church, what kind of a welcome do you give him? Sometime ago I was filling the pulpit of a church that had just called a new pastor. His wife and family were to arrive with him at the airport the next Friday evening. I suggested to the church family that as many as possible should plan to be at the airport to greet their new pastor and his family. Remarkably, more than 50 percent of that congregation showed up at the airport to form an official welcoming committee.

Imagine how encouraging that must have been for the new pastor. Returning missionaries need that same kind of encouragement. Do what the Jerusalem church did when Paul arrived. Receive your missionaries back with gladness and a little fanfare. They deserve it.

Uplift them after difficulties

Front-line missionaries are real people. Surprised? Sometimes we treat them like they're "supersaints," without normal problems or feelings. But even veteran missionaries occasionally have a difficult period of ministry. How can you encourage them?

Paul had been beaten by the Philippians and thrown into jail with Silas. After an earthquake there was an eight-point Richter Scale conversion that night. Great rejoicing followed. Still, it had been a difficult experience for Paul and Silas. Was there anything the behind-the-lines missionaries of Philippi could do to encourage them? There certainly was.

Acts 16:40 says, "So they went out of the prison and entered the house of Lydia; and when they had seen the brethren, they encouraged them and departed."

Doubtless Paul and Silas had to encourage the Philippian believers because of fear of what may happen to them as a result of the prison incident. But these two front-line missionaries needed some encouragement, too, and the Philippians were just the people to do it. They were the closest of all churches to the apostle Paul. They were the natural ones to encourage him when he needed it.

And who will encourage your missionary friends? If you don't, who will? Encouragement is a great behind-the-lines ministry. It's a valuable contribution you can make to the missionary enterprise around the world. Make the effort; make the contribution.

Write letters of support

One of the best ways to encourage front-line missionaries is by writing them letters. If you don't have the opportunity to visit them in person to encourage them, why not begin regular correspondence to encourage missionaries you know? It's always great to get news from home.

If you don't encourage your missionary friends, who will?

Paul wanted to confront paganism at Ephesus, but many Christians expressed their concerns about his plans. Acts 19:31 says that some of the officials of Asia Minor, who were his friends, even sent letters pleading with him not to go into the theater of Ephesus. There would surely be trouble.

It doesn't cost much to send a letter to a missionary—not nearly as much as it means to that front-line missionary. Send your church bulletin, clippings from the newspaper or Christian magazines or cassette tapes of messages that were particularly inspiring to you. Update your friends on what's going on. That's a way to encourage front-line missionaries from behind-the-lines.

The pen may be mightier than the sword, but today the word processor is mightier than the discouragement of distance. Keep that letter-link with your missionary friends. It's much more important to them than you may think.

Be present in times of need

Presence is the most powerful of all statements. Your mere presence with a retired missionary says to that faithful servant, "Thanks for serving the Lord so well. You are important to me, even now."

Think of all the times the New Testament pictures people, many of whose names we don't even know, lending support to the missionary enterprise around the world just by being there. When Paul was under house arrest in Rome, the last two verses of Acts say, "Then Paul dwelt two whole years in his own rented house, and received all who came to him, preaching the kingdom of God and teaching the things which concern the Lord Jesus Christ with all confidence, no one forbidding him" (28:30–31).

Imagine if Paul had been in a private dwelling for two years and no one came to see him. How would he have felt? Perhaps like a lot of retired missionaries who have returned from the field feel right now—neglected, unloved, unappreciated.

Your presence is a powerful statement of your appreciation. Paul commended Onesiphorus, who had come to Rome to minister to him behind-the-lines (2 Tim. 1:16). We don't know what Onesiphorus did exactly, but Paul said he often refreshed the sidelined missionary.

Paul had served the Lord faithfully and well. Now he was facing Nero's sword, and not many people encouraged him. But Onesiphorus did. What a wonderful ministry this man had as a behind-the-lines missionary.

Be an encourager like Barnabas, like the Ephesians, like the Philippians, like Onesiphorus. Don't miss your opportunity to be a genuine behind-the-lines missionary.

Conclusion

Not all of us are called to leave our homes and cross treacherous seas. All aren't even called to relocate in distant world capitals to plant a church. But we are all called to do something, and if we aren't sent as front-line missionaries, we gladly accept our calling to stay as behind-the-lines missionaries.

There's a place for you, Grandma, in the service of the Lord. There's a place for you, teenager. There's a place for you, young married couple, and you, Father, and you, Mother, and you and you and you. We are all saved for the same purpose—to serve the Lord (Eph. 2:10). Some of us are called to preach; others are called to teach. Some are called to go; others are called to sew. Some are called to sing in church choirs; others are called to wing their way to jungle stations.

What you are called to do is not the issue. The issue is are you doing what you are called to do? There is no shame in being a behind-the-lines missionary. The only shame is if you are a disobedient behind-the-lines missionary.

There's much more to the missionary enterprise than to give, go and pray. There's a whole life for you as a useful servant of God behind the lines. Find that abundant life in serving God right where you are. That's the kind of support that causes front-line missionaries to rejoice.

Back to the Bible is a nonprofit ministry dedicated to Bible teaching, evangelism and edification of Christians worldwide.

If we may assist you in knowing more about Christ and the Christian life, please write to us without obligation.

Back to the Bible
P.O. Box 82808
Lincoln, NE 68501

LINCOLN CHRISTIAN COLLEGE AND SEMINARY

266
K935

1039

3 4711 00169 2211